A DAY THAT MADE HISTORY

THE FIRST DAY OF THE SOMME

Richard Tames

Dryad Press   London

Contents

Acknowledgments

The author and publishers wish to thank the following for their kind permission to reproduce copyright illustrations: The Imperial War Museum for the frontispiece, and the illustrations on pages 5, 8, 12, 13, 14, 16, 19, 20, 22, 24, 30, 31, 32, 35, 36, 37, 38, 39, 40, 41, 42, 47, 48, 52, 55, 58, 59 and 62. The maps on pages 5, 10 and 25 were drawn by Robert Brien.

The cover illustrations are courtesy of The Imperial War Musuem.

The "Day that Made History" series was devised by Nathaniel Harris.

© Richard Tames 1990. First published 1990.
Typeset by Tek-Art Ltd, Kent, and printed and bound by Courier International, Tiptree, Essex for the publishers, Dryad Press, 4 Fitzhardinge Street, London W1H 0AH

ISBN 0 85219 829 9

THE
EVENTS

1st July, 1916

The plan was breathtakingly simple. Having assembled the greatest concentration of artillery in its entire history, the British army would bombard the German defences until their barbed wire was destroyed, their trenches caved in, their strong-points were smashed to fragments and the few remaining defenders were too stunned to fight. Then the British infantry, outnumbering the defenders seven to one and equipped with everything they could possibly require, would leave their own trenches, cross "No Man's Land" and calmly take possession.

It was to be the largest single action ever fought by a British army – 120,000 men attacking along an eighteen-mile front. And the army that would undertake this historic task was a new army – Kitchener's New Army, the best of Britain's manhood, hand-picked from half a million eager volunteers who had answered their country's call in the first few weeks of the war. Now they would end the war. This was to be "The Big Push", the day that would mark the beginning of the end for the Kaiser – 1st July, 1916.

The diary of the Reverend John Walker, a chaplain attached to the 21st Casualty Clearing Station, a few miles behind the British front line, reveals how the high hopes of the day were swiftly betrayed:

"Saturday 1 July 7.30 . . . the crazy hour had begun, every gun we owned fired as hard as ever it could for more than an hour . . . over us to left and right great observation balloons hung, eighteen in view. Aeroplanes dashed about, morning mist and gun smoke obscured the view. We got back for a late breakfast and soon the wounded by

German shells came in, then all day long cars of wounded and dying, but all cheerful, for they told us of a day of glorious successes. They are literally piled up – beds gone, lucky to get space on floor of tent, hut or ward and though the surgeons work like Trojans many must yet die for lack of operation. All the CCSs are overflowing.

Later. We have 1,500 in and still they come, 3-400 officers, it is a sight – chaps with fearful wounds lying in agony, many so patient, some make a noise, one goes to a stretcher, lays one's hand on the forehead, it is cold, strike a match, he is dead – here a Communion, there an absolution, there a drink, there a madman . . . it is an experience beside which all previous experience pales."
(Quoted in Moynihan (ed.), *People at War 1914-1918*)

Unfolding events

A battle is a complicated event, a big battle even more so. To get an overall picture of what happened on 1st July, 1916, let us follow the course of action right the way along the front, sector by sector, working from north to south.

The diversion

The most northerly sector of the British front was held by VII Corps, which formed part of the Third Army, commanded by General Allenby (see maps on page 10). VII Corps consisted of two divisions – the 46th (North Midland) and the 56th (London). Both were Territorial formations, recruited from pre-war part-time soldiers. Their task for 1st July was to launch a diversionary attack on the fortified village of Gommecourt, which jutted out toward the British lines on a spur of high ground and was defended by an excellent German division, the 2nd Guard Reserve.

In the words of their official instructions, VII Corps was "to assist in the operations of Fourth Army by diverting against itself the fire of artillery and infantry, which might otherwise be directed against the left flank of the main attack near Serre". Rather than undertake a frontal assault on Gommecourt, it was agreed that the two attacking divisions would advance on either side of the village and meet up round the rear, thus isolating it from possible reinforcement and hopefully obliging it to surrender.

Paths of glory. Neatly-spaced infantry pick their way through barbed wire obstacles.

Organizational structure of the British Army at the time of the Somme campaign.

The German and Allied front lines, June 1916.

	APPROX. NO. OF MEN	COMMANDED BY
ARMY	40,000 +	General
consists of 2 or more		
CORPS	20,000 men	Lt. Gen.
consists of 2 or more		
DIVISIONS	10 - 12,000 men	Maj. Gen.
consists of 3		
BRIGADES	3,500 - 4,000 men	Brig. Gen.
consists of 4		
BATTALIONS	800 - 1,000 men	Lt. Col.
consists of 4		
COMPANIES	160 - 200 men	Capt.
consists of 4		
PLATOONS	40 - 50 men	Lt.
consists of 4		
SECTIONS	10 - 14 men	Lance/Corporal

The 56th Division, attacking on the south side of Gommecourt, achieved substantial success at first. Faced with the problem of crossing 800 yards of "No Man's Land", the Londoners had prepared for the assault, under cover of night, by digging an entirely new front-line trench, half way across. It was 2,900 yards long and joined to their old front line by 1,500 yards of communication trenches. This had been accomplished in three nights by 3,000 men, with the loss of only eight dead and 55 wounded, thanks to the protection of patrols who had kept the Germans occupied.

On the morning of 1st July, with the additional cover of a smoke-screen laid down by the Royal Engineers, the first four battalions in the assault seized almost all of the German front-line trench system. Supported by Pioneers from the 1st/5th Cheshires, a fifth battalion, the Queen's Westminster Rifles, then attempted the second phase of the operation, passing through the captured lines in order to link up with the North Midlanders at the rear of Gommecourt. The Midlanders never got there, however, and the Westminsters and Pioneers fell back when they ran out of bombs to throw.

Meanwhile the Germans kept up an intense barrage of artillery fire, which effectively cut off the Londoners from their old front line. Out of 300 German prisoners whom the Londoners sent to the rear, only 178 arrived. The rest either escaped in the confusion or were killed by their own artillery.

By mid-day the Germans were able to counter-attack from three sides. They did so three times, and each time the attack was preceded by a short but intense bombardment. As the Londoners ran out of ammunition they were gradually forced back. By four o'clock in the afternoon they held only the front-line trench and were relying for ammunition on what they could find in the pouches of their dead compatriots. At nine in the evening a small party of five officers and 70 men was still holding out. Captain Sparks of the London Scottish, with four NCOs, armed with captured German rifles, then fought a final rearguard action while the rest of the men slipped away in gathering darkness.

The Londoners had lost everything they had gained – as well as 1,700 dead, 200 captured and 2,300 wounded, most of whom were still lying out in No Man's Land. The London Scottish had sent 871 men into battle and taken 616 casualties. The Queen's Westminster Rifles had lost every one of its 28 officers.

On the north side of Gommecourt, the 46th Division's attack had been a disaster from the start. Many of the men had had to spend the night in wet trenches and under heavy German shellfire. The smoke screen laid down to cover their advance added confusion to their discomfort. All six battalions in the assault were repulsed with heavy losses and five of their commanding officers killed or woulded. Only a few small parties of men even reached the German trenches and these were only forced back, killed or captured. So few returned that senior officers simply refused to believe that the rest could have been lost. Lt-Gen. Snow, commander of VII Corps, ordered a renewal of the attack in the afternoon. Major-General Stuart-Wortley, the commander of 46th Division, realized the hopelessness of the situation and ordered only a token effort, involving just two companies. In the end he cancelled even that, although one platoon did not receive the message, went ahead and lost every single man except the platoon sergeant.

Later a report came in that some of the Sherwood Foresters were holding out in German trenches. Two platoons of the 1st/5th Lincolns were sent out in the dark to find them and cover their retreat. It cost them 48 casualties, more than half their strength, to discover that the report was entirely mistaken.

On 5th July Major-General Stuart-Wortley was sent back to England. His refusal to order further suicidal attacks undoubtedly saved thousands of lives, but it cost him his career and he never held command of a combat unit again.

The action around Gommecourt, which resulted in nearly 7,000 casualties, was meant only as a diversion. From the point of view of the main attack it was irrelevant whether Gommecourt was taken or not. In that sense those deaths and maimings had served their purpose.

Gains lost

Divisions of the Fourth Army, commanded by General Rawlinson, were positioned in the next sectors of the front. The purpose of the most northerly unit, the 48th (South Midland) Division, was also to be diversionary. Fortunately for the 48th, its task was essentially passive. Two battalions were to man a two-mile stretch of front line and lay down a thick smoke-screen to confuse the Germans about the true direction of the main attack.

The most northerly major objective of the day was the village of Serre, and the responsibility for its capture was

Fatal delay. This mine detonated under the German redoubt at Beaumont Hamel was fired at 7.20 a.m., but the assault was held back for a further ten minutes.

assigned to the 31st Division, a unit consisting entirely of New Army battalions from the North of England. The Corps Commander, Lt-General Hunter-Weston, assured them that the artillery bombardment preceding the assault would be so powerful "that there would be no German trenches and all we had to do was walk into Serre". But the wire was not cut. Serre was not taken. And by ten o'clock in the morning it was all over, with two thirds of the men who had gone "over the top" lying dead or wounded in No Man's Land.

Beaumont Hamel was the next major objective to the south, another village fortress, protected by a huge defence work called Hawthorn Ridge. This was the target for the 4th and the 29th Divisions, both consisting largely of Regulars. The 4th Division had been more or less continuously in action since the battle of Mons in August 1914. The 29th had been at Gallipoli.

The attack on Beaumont Hamel would be preceded by the blowing of a massive mine, which would not only destroy the Hawthorn Ridge but also leave a vast crater which could be seized immediately as a strong-point. The mine was blown at 7.20 a.m. It took only minutes for the debris to settle, but the assault was not to begin until 7.30. Having been given such unmistakeable notice of the impending attack, the Germans, shaken but by no means disorganized, had ample time to position their machine-guns and call down a rain of artillery fire. One of their junior officers with the 109th Reserve Regiment remembered the moment vividly:

> "We heard the mines go up; then it was deathly quiet for a few moments. The English came walking, as though they were going to the theatre or as though they were on a parade ground. We felt they were mad. Our orders were given in complete calm and every man took careful aim to avoid wasting ammunition." (Quoted in Middlebrook, *The First Day on the Somme*)

By 8.30 a.m. the remanants of four English battalions had reached the German trenches and a single company was hanging on to the edge of the Hawthorn mine crater. At mid-morning two more battalions were ordered up to attack – the 1st Essex, experienced Regulars, and the 1st Newfoundland, a totally new unit and the only British Empire formation in the whole attack. The 752 Newfoundlanders had 300 yards to go before even reaching the British front line and 300 more to get across No Man's Land. Instead of threading their way through communications trenches they went straight over the top from a reserve trench, immediately exposing themselves to enemy fire. Within 40 minutes 91% had become casualties. The few who actually reached the German wire were shot when they got there. The Essex men, who worked their way methodically through the communications trenches, also failed to reach the German wire in strength, but at least they suffered only one third of the Newfoundlanders' terrible toll. Mercifully, no further attempts were made to renew the attack on Beaumont Hamel that day.

The "old sweats" of the 4th and 29th Divisions fought in vain. Not so their neighbours, the 36th (Ulster) Division. Recruited from the ranks of the (technically illegal) Protestant para-military Ulster Volunteer Force, these men took heart from the date assigned for their first battle. 1st July was the anniversary of the Battle of the Boyne.

Even before the action started, one Ulsterman was to display the sort of fearlessness that would make the whole division instantly famous. Billy McFadzean was working in a narrow assembly trench, one of a team of bombers preparing grenades. When a box of grenades fell over and toppled on to the floor of the trench he saw with horror that the pins had come out of two of them. Unhesitatingly he threw himself bodily over the box, taking the full force of the explosion. Billy's heroism cost him his life but saved everyone else in the trench. His was the first of four VCs won by the Ulstermen in the course of their first action.

The 36th Division was to attack north of Thiepval. Unlike many other units they had the advantage of thick cover close to their front line and were able to assemble in Thiepval Wood, out of sight of the Germans. Nor did they adopt the disciplined wave formations which were to cost others so dear. Instead they rushed forward, and found the wire well cut and the Germans slow to man their parapets. Unsupported on either flank, the Ulstermen advanced through heavy machine-gun fire to take the German front line and the Schwaben Redoubt, a heavily fortified position just behind it.

Here Captain Eric Bell won the division's second VC, throwing trench-mortar shells at the German defenders until he was killed at the head of a group of infantrymen who had lost their own officers and followed his lead. By mid-morning the Schwaben Redoubt was securely taken and 500 Germans had surrendered. The Ulstermen pushed on to their next objective – the German second-line trenches – but their

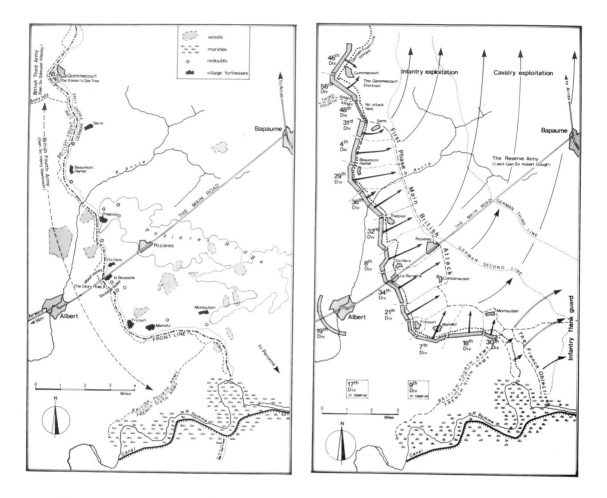

The Somme in June 1916.

advance had been so rapid that they had got ahead of the British artillery timetable which was advancing fire into German territory according to a strict series of timed "lifts". So they found themselves under their own fire as well as facing stiff German resistance. Fighting their very first battle, the Ulstermen were the only British troops anywhere that day to reach the German second line. Yet their very success put them in renewed danger. Far ahead of the units on either side of them, they could easily become cut off.

By mid-afternoon the Schwaben Redoubt was under German attack from three sides. Water was running low. Rifle cartridges were being used to keep the machine-guns going. At 3 o'clock, Lt-Col. Bowen of the 14th Irish Rifles tried to turn the weary defenders into reluctant heroes by threatening to shoot them himself:

Battle of the Somme: the Allied objectives and plan of attack.

". . . a lot of men from the 8th and 9th Royal Irish Rifles have broken under Bosch counter attack , . . . We had to stop them at revolver point and turn them back, a desperate show, the air stiff with shrapnel and terror-stricken men rushing blindly. These men did magnificently earlier in the day but they had reached the limit of their endurance." (Quoted in Middlebrook, *The First Day on the Somme*)

Yorkshire Territorials from the 49th Division, which had been held in reserve, were ordered up to relieve the Ulstermen, but the machine-gun fire from the direction of Thiepval village was so intense that they had to abandon their attempt to cross No Man's Land.

Throughout the long, hot afternoon the Germans pounded away with their artillery and launched three infantry counter-attacks. The Ulstermen beat them all off, but by evening their ammunition was exhausted and almost every officer a casualty. That night they withdrew from the Redoubt to the former German front line, which they finally managed to hand over to the West Yorks. It was precious territory, having cost 2,000 dead, 2,700 wounded and 165 taken prisoner. The Schwaben Redoubt was not to be in British hands again for another three months.

During the night, Lt Geoffrey Cather of the Armagh Volunteers brought in three wounded men. The following day, in full view of the enemy, he brought in another. He was killed by a German machine-gunner while giving water to a fifth wounded man. His was the third VC. The fourth went to Private Robert Quigg, batman to his former employer, Lt Sir Harry MacNaghten. He went into No Man's Land seven times in search of his officer and brought back a wounded man each time, until he was too exhausted to go out again. Sir Harry's body was never found.

Over the top. Infantry dash into action from a half-destroyed forward position. A staged version of events for the official film version of the Battle of the Somme.

Thiepval itself was the objective for the 32nd Division, another New Army unit, but "stiffened" by three battalions of Regulars. Its ranks included three battalions of men from Salford, another three from Glasgow (recruited respectively from the tramways, the Boys' Brigade and the city's shops and offices), one of Tyneside shopkeepers (the Newcastle Commercials) and another, the Lonsdales, recruited entirely from the Earl of Lonsdale's estates in the Carlisle area. The Glasgow Commercials' rush across No Man's Land enabled them to take part of the Leipzig Salient, but their success was isolated. The Newcastle Commercials began their advance in fine style, following a football kicked off by an ex-professional. However, they were cut down by machine-gun fire and had to endure the jeers of men of the 99th Reserve Regiment who stood up on their parapets to taunt the wounded. The Geordie lads had been told by their divisional Major Commander that, "You will be able to go over the top with a walking stick. You will not need rifles. When you get to Thiepval you will find the Germans all dead. Not even a rat will have survived." In all, the division suffered just short of 4000 casualties. Thiepval was not taken for another 89 days.

Dead centre

The centre of the British attack, entrusted to III Corps, was to take place along the line of the old Roman road which ran in a dead straight line from Albert, some two miles behind the British lines, to Bapaume, nine miles behind the German line. Bapaume was the major intermediate objective, to be taken by three divisions of cavalry which would charge through the gap created by the initial assault. To the left (north) of the road the 8th Division, Regulars with a single Kitchener brigade, would aim for the fortified village of

Softening up. A rare picture of the German lines actually under fire.

Ovillers and, beyond that, Pozières. On the right (south) the 34th, an entirely New Army formation, would storm the ruined hamlet at La Boisselle. The 19th (Western) Division would stay in reserve at Albert and then, when Pozières had been taken, move through with the cavalry and secure Bapaume.

Few of the 8th Division ever got within shooting distance of Ovillers. At the cost of 5,121 killed and wounded, they inflicted just 280 casualties on its German defenders.

The fate of the 34th Division was even more horrendous. All four colonels of the Tyneside Scottish were killed leading their men. Indeed, the 1st and 4th battalions were virtually wiped out. The 15th and 16th Royal Scots (nominally an Edinburgh regiment but mostly, in fact, from Manchester) lost hundreds to machine-gun fire but did get to the German lines, as did the 10th Lincolns (Grimsby Chums) and 11th Suffolks (Cambridge Battalion). According to the Official History commissioned by the British government to tell the story of the war, those who did get that far "were burnt to death by flame throwers". The 103rd Brigade, four battalions of Tyneside-Irish, who were supposed to act as a reserve, were ordered up in support of the attack so soon that they were forced to cross a mile of open ground, swept by machine-gun fire, before they even reached the British front line. Most didn't, dying on territory that was British before the battle had even begun.

To the 21st Division and the 50th Brigade of the 17th Division, which was attached to the 21st for the day, fell the task of capturing Fricourt. The 21st was typical of the New Army, in that every one of its battalion commanders had been retired when the war broke out and only fourteen of its other officers had any military experience at all. The remaining 400 were all newly commissioned and mostly without any substantial officer training. The day began promisingly

Walking ducks. Tyneside Irish silhouetted against a skyline made an easy target for machine-gunners.

enough, with a bold rush by the 9th and 10th King's Own Yorkshire Light Infantry who defied heavy losses from machine-gun fire to seize the German front-line trench and 200 prisoners with it. All this in ten minutes – but at the cost of half their men and almost all their officers. After half an hour the advance ground to a halt in the face of German resistance. Throughout the rest of the day German counter-attacks were thrown back, but at nightfall the British withdrew to their own lines, having lost over 5,000 men. The 10th West Yorks achieved the hideous distinction of suffering more casualties than any other single battalion in action that day – 22 officers and 688 men.

The 7th Division, Regulars with a Kitchener brigade thrown in for good measure, were assigned to take Mametz. They had already seen much hard fighting and were fortunate that their commander, Major-General Watts, unlike so many that day, did not hesitate to alter the plan as circumstances changed. Having captured the German front-line trenches, the 7th were held up by the defenders of Mametz itself. Watts ordered the attackers to halt, ordered a new bombardment and sent in fresh troops to take over the lead. This he did three times. After bitter hand-to-hand fighting, the village fell to a combination of Manchesters and Devons in the late afternoon.

First of the few. British Tommies escort wounded German prisoners to a safe rear area.

Success in the south

The extreme right of the British line was held by the 18th (Eastern) and 30th Divisions, both New Army formations. Their objective was Montauban. And they took it.

The 30th consisted of four Liverpool and four Manchester battalions, plus four battalions of Regulars, who had been in France since 1914. The initial attack was completely successful, with three Liverpool Pals' and one Manchester battalion taking the whole German front line. The village of Montauban itself was then stormed by two more Manchester battalions, backed up by the 2nd Royal Scots Fusiliers. A single German machine-gun took a heavy toll of the attackers before it was knocked out. All the leading British company commanders were killed or badly wounded and the neat formations of men dissolved into two mobs who charged into the ruins of the village. Its defenders then swiftly surrendered. The Scots Fusiliers rounded up 200 prisoners from the cellars of surviving houses and trenches, while the Manchesters swept on to take a further German trench, Montauban Alley, immediately in the rear of the village, where they halted to fire at more fleeing Germans and seized three field guns.

The 30th was the only one of the thirteen assaulting divisions to take and hold all of its objectives during the morning. On 4th July it would be withdrawn for a well-earned rest. It had gained such a fine reputation that it would be used again and again as a "stormer" – until at last it became so depleted that it was temporarily disbanded.

The 18th, supporting the 30th on its left, was fortunate to be commanded by Major-General Maxse, a tough but experienced tactician who believed in training men until they were ready to drop. His front-line troops – the 18th Norfolks, 7th Queens' and 8th East Surrey – had never been in a battle before and he was determined to adapt his tactics to take account of their inexperience. Ordering his men out into No Man's Land before the British bombardment had ended, he warned them that they must be prepared to accept 6% casualties from British "shortfalls" in return for getting close to the enemy. The defenders of Breslau trench fell to their first rush.

This southernmost sector, from Fricourt to where the British line joined the French, achieved the nearest to what one could call success on the whole British front. Even so, the 18th and 30th Divisions between them suffered more than 6,000 casualties.

The balance sheet

When night fell on the Somme front, the British were in possession of three fortified villages Montauban, Mametz and Fricourt. Strictly speaking it was only two, for Fricourt was only finally abandoned by the Germans during the night. The plan had been to take 13 such positions. At no point had the German second line been breached.

These gains had cost a total of 57,470 casualties – almost half the men involved in the attack. 585 had been taken prisoner, 2,152 were listed as missing, 35,493 had been wounded and no fewer than 19,240, a third of the total, were either killed outright or wounded so seriously that they were to die within days. Three quarters of all the officers who had gone into action had become casualties – 2,438 of them. British losses on the first day of the Somme exceeded the battle casualties of the Crimean war, the Boer war and the Korean war – *added together*. It had been the biggest single battle ever fought by an all-British army and, in terms of casualties, a disaster without precedent or successor.

'For you the war is over.' German and British wounded lie side-by-side awaiting evacuation.

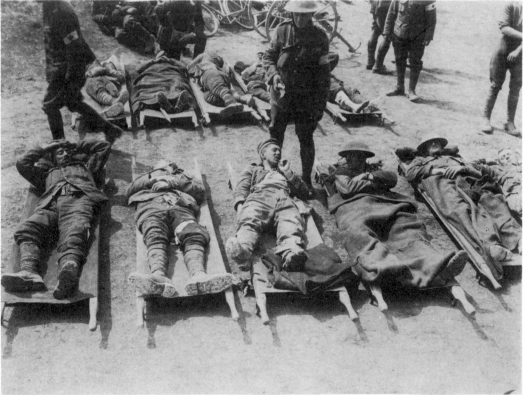

Slogging on

It took days for the full enormity of the catastrophe to sink in. On 2nd July at Fourth Army headquarters estimates of the casualties of the previous day's fighting were still 40% below the actual figures. At 10.00 p.m. some 10,000 of the first day's wounded were still in the battle zone and, of these, half had still not received any trained medical attention.

At 21st Casualty Clearing Station, the Rev. John Walker recorded in his diary on 3rd July:

> "Now I know something of the horrors of war . . . . The surgeons are beginning to get sleep, because after working night and day they realise we may be at this for some months . . . . We hear of great successes but there are of course setbacks and one hears of ramparts of dead English and Germans. Oh, if you could see our wards, tents, huts, crammed with terrible wounds . . .
>
> . . . in strict confidence . . . I got hold of some morphia . . . I creep into the long tents where two or three hundred Germans lie; you can imagine what attention they get with our own neglected, the cries and groans are too much to withstand and I cannot feel less pity for them than for our own. Surgeons and sisters are splendid and I go and bother them and they come without grumbling. But one cannot drag them away from life-saving to death-easing too often." (Quoted in Moynihan (ed.), *People at War 1914-1918*)

Ironically, the sacrifices of 1st July, which arose largely because attacks were pressed where they were hopeless, were thrown away in the confusion of 2nd July, when continued pressure might have paid off. The German front line had been severely jolted and the German High Command was still confused about the nature and precise direction of the attack. However, chaos behind the British lines, as the wounded streamed back and reinforcements tried to pass forward, made a determined follow-through impossible.

For ten days the British Higher Command dithered, acknowledging front-line commanders' reports that a full-scale renewal of the frontal assault was impossible, but determined to find some means of exploiting the gains that had been made. The result was a series of small-scale and unco-ordinated attacks which achieved little other than adding to the list of casualties. Ovillers was entered on 3rd July, after a confused struggle, by men of five different battalions. Cut off from reinforcements and re-supply, they were annihilated – another 2,400 men lost. The net outcome of this indecision was to give the Germans a breathing space in which to regroup their forces and reorganize their defences, especially in the south, between Montauban and La Boisselle, where they had been forced out of their prepared positions.

Realizing that an effort would have to be made to resume the offensive – or else this major effort would have to be abandoned – the British Higher Command resolved to attack again in strength, but on a much narrower front. They would focus on the area between Delville Wood and Bazentin-le-Petit Wood, and use radically different tactics – a rediscovery of the oldest trick in the military book: surprise. This time the troops were to cross the exposed area under cover of darkness; then, after a violent but *brief* bombardment, they were to launch a rush attack in the half-light of dawn. Orthodox army opinion held that a night operation would be beyond the capabilities of New Army men, not real soldiers but civilians in uniform, and that the result would be a complete shambles. Fortunately, bolder counsels prevailed.

The German front line on the target sector was thinly held by six battalions and these were from different divisions, unused to working together. At 3.20 a.m. on 14th July, the Germans reeled under the sudden onslaught of an intense bombardment. Five minutes later the shelling stopped and the British infantry were upon them, seizing four miles of the German line to a depth of 1,000 yards.

By the evening, the 21st Division had taken Bazentin-le-Petit Wood, the 7th Bazentin-le-Grand Wood, the 3rd Bazentin-le-Grand itself and the 9th Longueval. Beyond Longueval lay Delville Wood. The South African Brigade went in 3,000 strong and took it. When they were relieved and came out, 768 were left to answer the roll. Of their 2,000 odd casualties the dead outnumbered the wounded by four to one. In a "normal" battle these figures would have been reversed. None of the South Africans had been taken prisoner.

North of the road from Longueval to Martinpuich lay High Wood, from which the Germans could look down over miles of the British front. By nightfall all but a corner of that, too, was in British hands.

But the advantage was not pressed home. Nine precious hours were wasted before senior officers in the rear had a clear enough grasp of the situation to see the opportunity for exploiting it. By that time the Germans had brought up fresh reserves and on 15th July forced the British out of High Wood. It was to take two months and much bloody fighting before it was regained.

For the next six weeks, repeated, if limited, attacks were made to press further forward by "nibbling away" at the German defences. The gain was a tiny tongue of ground just over one mile deep. The cost was 23,000 men. At Pozières, taken by the Australians between 23rd and 29th July, the dead lay more thickly upon the ground than upon any other battlefield of the entire war.

The onset of autumn concentrated British minds on the need to achieve a decisive result before wet weather made further offensive action impossible. Accordingly, the British committed themselves to a mid-September thrust against what had originally been the Germans' rear defences, between Morval and Le Sars. If successful, this was to be developed by reserve troops into a breakthrough and the seizure of Courcelette and Martinpuich.

The attack, launched at dawn on 15th September, was preceded by a three-day bombardment. Eight divisions took part in the assault, which was aided by a morning mist. Even more helpful was the effect of the new British secret weapon – the tank, dismissed by Kitchener in 1915 as "a pretty mechanical toy but of very limited military value". This was not what the troops thought. Rumours about this technological marvel had swept ahead of it. Bernard Martin, a lieutenant with the North Staffs, assured his fellow officers that Britain had at last turned the tables:

Wasteland. Infantry trudge through a devastated landscape near La Boisselle, November 1916.

"Bosch have always been ahead of us, first to use cloud-gas, first with flame-throwers, better aircraft than the flying corps, more guns than the RA, ten times more machine-guns and we've only just caught up from the shell shortage . . . that's past history. Now we've a new weapon; going to make history . . . a real breakthrough . . . end the war quickly." (Bernard Martin, *Poor Bloody Infantry*)

It did, in the long run, make history, but it did not end the war quickly.

The tank had been developed thanks largely to the far-sightedness of Winston Churchill, First Lord of the Admiralty, and his willingness to use navy funds for its perfection. Perfection had not, however, been achieved by the time the army, desperate for some means of victory, was converted to the view that this "land battleship" was a potential war-winning weapon which could break the trench-war stalemate on the Western Front. Anxious to redeem the sacrifices of the Somme offensive, the British Higher Command decided to press the tanks into service, despite warnings that their crews were still untrained and the vehicles themselves far from ready for the ultimate test of battle.

Only 60 tanks were actually available in France and of these only 32 could be prepared for action. Five got stranded in craters on the battlefield. Nine broke down with engine, steering or other mechanical failures. Nine failed to catch up with the advancing infantry. But nine did keep up, and their impact was out of all proportion to their number. A German regimental history conceded that:

"The arrival of the tanks on the scene had the most shattering effect on the men. They felt quite powerless against these monsters which crawled along the top of the

War-winner? The first official photograph of a tank going into action, Flers, 15 September 1916.

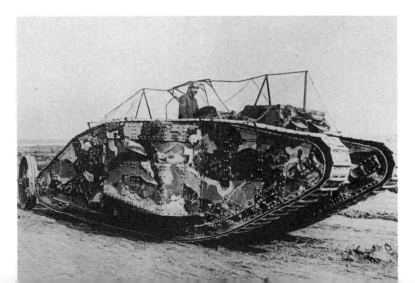

trench, enfilading it with continuous machine-gun fire, and closely followed by small parties of infantry who threw hand grenades on the survivors." (Quoted in Captain Sir Basil Liddell Hart, *History of the First World War*)

XV Corps, in the centre of the British attack, took Flers by 10.00 a.m. The cheering forward troops swaggered behind a tank as it rumbled through what was left of the High Street. Then they pressed on. III Corps, on the left, finally cleared out High Wood and, on the extreme left, both Martinpuich and Courcelette were also taken. XIV Corps on the right, however, lost heavily and failed to reach Morval. Nevertheless, by the end of the day, the British held most of the ridge from which, for so long, the Germans had looked and fired down upon them.

Again, success had been dearly bought. Lt William St Leger of the Coldstream Guards wrote in his diary on 21st September:

> "The battlefield of the 15th is a ghastly sight. The ground is simply pitted with shell-holes, dead men lie here and there, heads towards the enemy, and nearly every one lying on his face. The moon, peeping occasionally from behind the clouds, shines pitilessly down upon this treeless, devastated, god-forsaken land of the dead and everywhere is the stench, somewhere faint, somewhere strong. It all looks so sad and one thinks of all the homes to which these brave men will never return." (Quoted in Moynihan (ed.), *People at War 1914-1918*)

The right of the ridge was finally taken by a big attack on 25th September, which forced the Germans out of Combles. On the following day Thiepval finally fell to an assault by four divisions – and three tanks, which appear to have done the trick.

The British kept up the pressure and, by the first week of October, the Germans were holding on to their last completed line of defences, which ran from Sailly-Sallisel past Le Transloy and in front of Bapaume. To the rear of this line they feverishly constructed a further series of fortifications. Meanwhile the rain had arrived. Combined with continued artillery bombardment, this made the ground a morass which bogged down not only heavy guns and supply waggons but even lightly equipped infantry. To move wheeled traffic within three miles of the front was all but impossible. The

Nature also bears the scars. Beaumont Hamel, November 1916.

hope that any break in the German lines could be followed by a rapid advance soon became quite unrealistic. During October the British took another 60,000 casualties.

The pressure was maintained through a series of small-scale actions until 13th November, when a brief improvement in the weather allowed seven divisions to mount a last major effort. This resulted in the capture of Beaumont Hamel, Beaucourt-sur-Ancre and 7,000 prisoners. But Serre, the 31st Division's objective on the very first day of the offensive, still defied all attempts to take it.

It was 141 days since the "Battle of the Somme" had begun. British General Headquarters estimated their casualties at 460,000, a figure later corrected to 415,000. The French, attacking to the south, had lost 195,000. The German figures were less easy to be sure of because the Germans had begun to conceal the true extent of the damage they had suffered. Perhaps this was some consolation for the price that the British had paid.

In describing conditions on the Somme front during the period of the offensive, the British "Official History" of the war, a publication notable for its lack of emotion, was to conclude bleakly:

"Our vocabulary is not adapted to describe such an existence, because it is outside experience for which words are normally required."

From Arras to Armistice

1916 had not been the year of decision for Britain and its Allies. 1917 was to be for them a year of endurance. This year's great gain was the United States' entry into the war on the Allied side and all that this promised in terms of man-power and wealth. However, it would take time for America's strength to be brought to bear. In the meantime, the Allied cause endured a series of hammer-blows: revolution in Russia, which finally forced that immense reservoir of man-power out of the war; mutiny in the French army; the collapse and wholesale flight of Italy's forces on the Isonzo front against Austria; and the German conquest of Romania, with its supplies of oil and wheat.

Confident that they had learned the lessons of 1916, the Allied generals launched further offensives on the Western Front. In April 1917 the British attacked at Arras. The Canadians took Vimy Ridge, an important vantage point. But total losses were 84,000 men and the gains only a few miles. In the same month the French attacked along the line of the river Aisne, after a bombardment of 11,000,000 shells. Again, little was gained and 120,000 men were lost. It was this failure which led to the mutinies that obliged the British then to take up the entire burden of offensive action. The outcome was the battle of Passchendaele. In theory, this battle was an attempt to break through the German front and seize the Belgian Channel ports. In practice, the immense bombardment before the attack simply destroyed the drainage system of an area which heavy rains soon reduced to an impassable quagmire. Some territory was gained, and another 360,000 men were lost.

As far as the Western Front was concerned, the year did, however, end on a note of promise. At Cambrai, in late November, the British launched an attack with five divisions and 324 tanks. 179 of the tanks were knocked out or otherwise disabled, but the advance penetrated to the last German defence line. Most of the ground gained was lost to a counter-attack within a matter of days, but the potential of the tank had at last been proved beyond doubt.

With Russia out of the war, the German High Command felt that the spring of 1918 offered them a last chance to end the conflict by a decisive offensive on the Western Front –

before the Americans arrived in force. The attack would be made on a 40-mile front, but the primary objective was the area where the British and French armies joined – near Amiens and the Somme. The tactics would combine a short but devastating barrage with a swift onslaught by specially trained and selected "storm-troopers". These men would operate as small units and simply by-pass any strong-points of resistance which they could not knock out, leaving them to be dealt with by regular forces afterwards. The Allies knew that an attack was coming, but the ferocity of the bombardment launched on 21st March simply overwhelmed them. Within four days, the Germans had advanced 14 miles and were threatening the vital rail junction at Amiens. Having suffered 230,000 casualties, the Allies at last agreed that there should be a single overall director of their resistance and hurriedly appointed General (later Marshal) Foch to that unenviable position.

The Germans then launched a second initiative near Ypres, aiming at the railway junction at Hazebrouck and beyond that at the Channel ports, the British Expeditionary Force's lifeline to England. The British troops facing this new menace received the following communication from their commander-in-chief Haig: "There is no other course open to us but to fight it out. Every position must be held to the last man. With our backs to the wall, and believing in the justice of our cause, each one must fight on to the end."

With the aid of reinforcements, the German advance was held back. But the tide had not yet turned. On 27th May the Germans struck again on a 25-mile front in the region of the river Aisne. By 3rd June they were little more than 50 miles from Paris. Another thrust on 9th June gained them a further six miles. On 15th July they made their final attempt and crossed the Marne, only to be driven back by a crushing French counter-attack. For the Germans, that was the

Afterwards. Guillemont, September 1916.

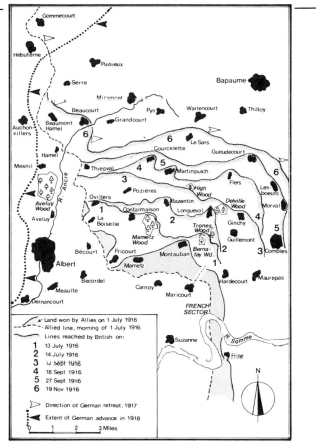

The Somme, 1916-1918.

beginning of the end. They had taken 250,000 prisoners and inflicted a million casualties – but they had reached their last gasp. The gamble had failed.

By July there were 29 American divisions in France and the Allies could launch a counter-offensive. 8th August proved to be the crucial day, when combined Allied forces launched a determined assault in the Amiens-Somme area. Led by 456 tanks, they seized 400 guns and inflicted 42,000 casualties. It was, for the Germans, "the blackest day" and the final turning-point of the war. Thereafter their armies were entirely on the defensive, at the mercy of well-co-ordinated Allied attacks, which hit now one part of the German line, now another, making it impossible for the High Command to use its last reserves to good effect.

By October the German position was clearly hopeless, the High Command discredited, the navy in a state of mutiny and the half-starved civilian population rioting on the streets. On 9th November the Kaiser fled to neutral Holland. On 11th November the new republican German government accepted the Allied terms for an armistice. The war was over.

THE INVESTIGATION

Why was the British plan a disaster?

Why did Britain go to war?

Britain declared war on Germany on 4th August, 1914. Germany had invaded France, with whom Britain had no formal treaty of alliance but rather a ten-year-old "entente", or understanding, that, in the event of a Franco-German conflict, Britain would come in on the French side. More to the point, the German war plan required part of her army to march through neutral Belgium. According to the Treaty of London, 1839, which had established Belgium as an independent state, both Britain and Germany were guarantors of the little country's "territorial integrity" – that is, they were bound to protect it from such a violation.

Britain could thus proclaim her prime war aim in high moral terms: the rescue of a small, peace-loving nation and the punishment of an unprincipled bully. The savagery of the German assault on Belgium's frontier defences and the brutality of the invading troops towards the civilian population provided further vindication of the British point of view. The "rape of Belgium" turned a war into a crusade.

Of course, there was more to it than that. British strategic interests had always dictated the desirability of the Low Countries being under the control of weak, neutral states rather than well-armed and predatory ones. The coast-line of that part of north-west Europe was, after all, the obvious jumping-off point for an invasion of Britain. The neutrality of Belgium was, therefore, not merely a matter of abstract principle but also important for Britain's national security – which is why Britain had been prime mover in creating an independent Belgium in the first place.

There was also the powerful factor of anti-German feeling. The British did not, on the whole, think highly of any

European people; but they regarded the Germans with suspicion rather than mere contempt. Germany's industries were outstripping Britain's in both output and technical advance. Goods "made in Germany" offered fierce competition to those of British manufacturers, and this threatened British workers' jobs. Germany, moreover, had for a quarter of a century been building a great navy. Why should Europe's best-armed land-power need one; except to attack the British Empire? For more reasons than one, the average Briton thought that Germany ought to be put in her place, and the government's decision for war was therefore met with enthusiastic public support.

How would the war be won? The expectation among many experts, and most ordinary people who gave the matter a thought, was that the conflict would be settled by a single passage of arms. Europe had known no major war for almost half a century – numerous colonial campaigns excepted, of course; but they were fought by professional armies, and far, far away. The Franco-Prussian war of 1870-71, which had effectively been settled in the first few weeks of fighting, was still widely regarded as the model of modern warfare. Few people seem to have realized that the four-year slogging-match of the American Civil War (1861-65) would be much nearer the mark. The war against Germany, it was generally believed, would be "over by Christmas", and young men rushed to volunteer, lest they should be too late to give "Kaiser Bill" a good thrashing.

The outcome of a decade of "military conversations" with the French had been an agreement that the outbreak of a Franco-German war would be followed by the swift despatch of a British Expeditionary Force (BEF) of six divisions of infantry and one of cavalry, which would take up their position beside the French to beat back the invader. It is probable that the French regarded such co-operation as being of more political than military value: the British troops would be an unambiguous indication to the aggressor of British support, rather than a vital ingredient in French security. Britain's real strength was her sea-power, and her strategic contribution would surely be to act as a counter-weight to the German navy and, in the event of an extended conflict, to blockade Germany's ports.

Britain's army was trained and equipped to a high standard and had undergone many recent reforms in the light of the painful experiences of the Boer War (1899-1902); but it was, by continental standards, insignificant. Both Germany and

France could readily put 2,000,000 men in the field, Britain barely 100,000. This comparison, however, did little to diminish British pride. The mass of every continental army was made up of conscripts. The British, by contrast, were volunteers to a man, professionals, a caste apart. When it was said that Kaiser Wilhelm II had referred to the BEF as "that contemptible little army", they appropriated the reference with perverse pride and ever after referred to themselves as the "Old Contemptibles".

How did the war become a stale-mate? Having been escorted safely across the Channel by the Royal Navy, the BEF immediately found itself pitched into a fighting retreat as the French reeled back before Germany's meticulously prepared invasion. The Germans, as the aggressors, had taken the initiative and set the terms on which the fighting was to take place. Their master-plan required a swift knock-out victory over France before France's ally, Russia, could fully mobilize her immense army of 5,000,000 men. The German intention was to seize Paris – which, they assumed, would force the French to surrender – and then turn east to deal with the Russians at their leisure. At all costs they wished to avoid fighting on two fronts simultaneously.

At first, all had gone well for them. They had swept aside Belgian resistance and captured that country's Channel ports. They had advanced deep into France, threatening Paris itself. But they had been stopped. Along the line of the river Marne, dogged Franco-British resistance finally brought the Germans to a halt.

Each side then attempted to turn the other's open flank in an effort to get behind their opponents and squeeze them from both sides. Neither could out-run the other and the unlooked-for outcome of the "race for the sea" was two sets of hastily-constructed trenches which stretched from the Belgian coast to Switzerland. As winter drew on, it became clear that neither side would achieve victory by Christmas. Both settled down to make themselves as comfortable as possible. The Germans elaborated their defences. The French and British pondered how to dislodge them when spring made campaigning possible again.

The Allies try to break the stale-mate The onus was clearly on France and her allies to make the next move. The invader had gained territory and had only to hold it to claim victory. It was up to the Allies to regain that territory by forcing the Germans out of their defences.

The campaigns of 1915 opened with a British attack in

March at Neuve Chapelle. The Germans countered in April by attacking Ypres – their only offensive of the year. Further Allied efforts followed, culminating in the battle of Loos in September. It cost the French a million casualties and the British 300,000 in that year to learn that old-style "open warfare", with skilful manoeuvres by the infantry and sweeping movements by the cavalry, was a thing of the past. It had cost the Germans 700,000 casualties to teach them that lesson. There were those who believed that full-frontal collision on the Western Front was not the only possible way of beating Germany. These "Easterners" placed their faith in an expedition to force the Dardanelles, the waterway between the Mediterranean and the Black Sea, thus opening up a Black Sea supply route to Russia and possibly even knocking the Ottoman Empire, Germany's ally, out of the war. Alas, the disastrous campaign to seize the Gallipoli peninsula revealed that the Turks were much better fighters than they had been given credit for, and amphibious operations much more difficult to carry out than anyone had foreseen. More hard lessons at the price of another 250,000 casualties. As 1915 drew to a close, Allied strategy focused again on the Western Front. It was here and, Gallipoli seemed to prove, here alone, that Germany would be beaten. The problem was – how?

The Allied plan evolves 1916 was intended by the Allies to be the year of victory over Germany. Victory would be achieved by mounting three simultaneous offensives – a Russian one in the east, an Italian one in the south and a Franco-British one in the west.

In December 1915 the British and French generals met at Chantilly to plan their offensive. Heading the French delegation was General Joffre, Chief-of-Staff since 1911, while the British were led by the newly appointed Commander-in-Chief of the BEF, General Sir Douglas Haig. The two men had certain qualities in common. Both had a reputation for a cool head in a crisis. And both had gained their practical experience of warfare in colonial campaigns, in which European troops had used modern weapons against enemies who were not as well-armed, well-fed, well-led or well-organized. This time it would be different.

Thanks to Haig's good command of French, the two men could communicate easily. However, they were uneasy in their partnership. Haig was aware that, fighting on French soil, the British perforce depended on their ally for many services and supplies. On land at least, the British were the

Sir Douglas Haig (centre), with his French allies General Joffre (left) and General Foch (right).

junior partners in the alliance, the French army being so much the larger and, in many respects, more experienced. Joffre, for his part, was only too aware that it was the French army which had done the bulk of the fighting, and dying, so far. His major objective was to get the British to commit their rapidly expanding army to take a far greater share of the burden.

Haig's original preference was for another offensive in Flanders, combined with a sea-borne landing along the coast. Joffre wanted the Somme. Why? Simply because it was here that the British and French armies joined. If there were two separate offensives at different points in the line, how could the French prevent their ally breaking off if the going got rough? Having no direct common authority, they could not. But if the two armies attacked quite literally side by side, their fates would be inextricably cast together. The British "Official History" was to note testily, after the war, that the French preference for an offensive on the Somme "seems to have been arrived at solely because the British would be bound to take part in it. The reasons advanced by General Joffre will hardly bear examination."

Haig eventually gave way. He was eager to prove himself and realized that, even though he would have far more troops at his disposal than his predecessor had had, he could not beat the Germans without French support. If the price was an attack on the Somme, so be it. Joffre, having won his main point, gave up his preference for a series of preliminary assaults to drain the Germans of reserves, in deference to

Haig's conviction that there should be a single massive effort. At this stage it was agreed that the French would contribute 39 divisions to the joint enterprise, the British 25 or even 30. By early February the broad outlines of the scheme were settled. Only the precise date had yet to be determined.

Taken by surprise Then the Germans struck at Verdun. The Chief of the German General Staff, von Falkenhayn, reasoned that the French army had already been gravely weakened by the huge casualties of 1915, resulting from the French military doctrine of all-out attack. They could now be "bled white" by being forced to defend, at all costs, the frontier fortress city of Verdun, the scene of humiliating defeat in the war of 1870-71.

The battle for Verdun began on 21st February, 1916. Von Falkenhayn's psychology was right, but his mathematics were wrong. The French did feel obliged to defend Verdun at all costs, and were to take 315,000 casualties doing so. But the Germans were to lose almost as many – 281,000. Bleeding the French white only made sense if it did not mean bleeding the Germans white as well. In strategic terms, the slaughter was pointless. Possession of Verdun would give a vital advantage to neither side.

The struggle for Verdun did have a decisive effect on the plans for the Somme offensive, however. Within days of its beginning, Haig ordered British troops to take over sections of the French line, releasing the French to go south to meet

The warlords. German generals consider their strategy. Von Falkenhayn is in the centre

their fate. The British who should have been training for their own trial of strength were thus increasingly exposed to the constant drain of trench warfare, which cost the average battalion one man a day through snipers, accidents and sickness. It soon became apparent that the original plan for an offensive along the Somme would have to be drastically revised in two fundamental aspects – the scale of the French contribution and the actual date of the attack.

The French made it clear that they could no longer offer 39 divisions; 18 would have to suffice. The British would now bear the main burden of the enterprise. Haig's own role as commander would thus be much more prominent, which presumably did not displease him. At any rate he did not suggest calling off the planned operation, although he did revise his expectations of it. In May he told his army commanders that the summer offensive could no longer be expected to create a breakthrough, leading to immediate victory. Instead its objects were now three-fold: to take the pressure off the French at Verdun; to inflict losses upon the Germans; and to advance the British army to positions from which they could achieve decisive success in 1917. Another motive may well have been simply to make visible Britain's continued commitment to the fight. On 23rd May, General Sir Henry Rawlinson, commander of the Fourth Army, confided to his diary: "There are rumours of peace amongst the politicians, so it will be as well to have a go before they can mature."

Rawlinson (left) and Haig outside Allied Head-quarters, July 1916.

As far as the date of the attack was concerned, French demands for a mid-summer action became increasingly strident as the fighting around Verdun became more desperate. On 26th May Joffre confronted Haig in person and told him that if the British waited until August "the French army would cease to exist". Haig then offered 1st July as a firm date. Five days later, as a result of the personal intervention of the French President, Poincaré, Haig agreed to bring the date forward to 25th June. By mid-June, however, the French conceded that the crisis at Verdun had passed and Haig revised the date again, to 29th June. (In the event bad weather was to lead to a two-day postponement of the actual assault.)

With the improvement of the situation at Verdun, the reasons for an offensive on the Somme seem even more obscure. The urgent need to relieve the French had disappeared. There was no great strategic prize behind the German lines, no supply-depot or railway-junction. Even the justification that a Somme operation would enable the British and French to co-operate as equal partners no longer had any validity, for the French contribution would be further and further reduced until, on the actual day, only five divisions took part. Perhaps they went ahead simply because this was one part of the line where an attack had not yet been tried and failed. Whatever the reason, since the plan had first been made, its purpose had changed, the strengths of the participants had changed, and even the nature of the terrain had changed.

Why the landscape was important

"What first struck me was the very different kind of country about us – instead of the flat Flanders plain, with straight tree-lined roads and hedged farmland, the river Somme and its tributaries ran through gentle valleys in undulating country, with low hills rising to ridges or plateaux, set about with numerous small woods and fields with hedges." (Bernard Martin, _Poor Bloody Infantry_)

The contrast between Flanders and Picardy was striking to the young Lieutenant Bernard Martin. Many of his fellow officers thought that the Somme area reminded them of the Sussex Downs. Others were struck by a different contrast between Flanders and Picardy: whereas the Belgian sector had always been a "lively" one, the area chosen for the great offensive had a reputation as "quiet", with little action between the opposing sides.

The arrival of the British in July 1915 changed all that. Their generals believed that the "live and let live" attitude towards each other of some French and German units between major offensives was bad for morale. It was important to "keep the men on their toes" and always let the enemy "know there's a war on". Night patrols to throw bombs, snatch prisoners for interrogation or simply to deprive the enemy of rest and of the chance to repair his trenches, were felt to be the best methods of achieving these general objectives.

They also had another effect – provoking the Germans into greatly strengthening their defences. Using Russian prisoners as labourers, the Germans constructed no fewer than four lines of trenches, each consisting of a forward, support and reserve trench. Hugging the high ground, they looked down on their British besiegers for miles. As the poet John Masefield was to observe in his book *The Old Front Line*:

> "Almost in every part of this old front our men had to go up hill to attack . . . . The enemy had the look-out posts, with the fine views . . . and the sense of domination. Our men were down below, with no view of anything but of stronghold after stronghold, just up above, being made stronger daily."

There was more going on that the British infantry could not see, although some of them were perceptive enough to guess. As Bernard Martin acutely observed:

> "Infantry live in the open, with makeshift shelters, so the nature of the soil is important. The Somme country is chalk to a great depth. The first trenches I saw, just captured from the enemy, were dry, strong in construction, with steps going down about fifteen feet underground into large dug-outs giving complete protection from gunfire . . ."
> (Bernard Martin, *Poor Bloody Infantry*)

Some German dug-outs went down as far as 40 feet and even had such luxuries as electric lighting, piped water, ventilation systems and wood-panelled walls. Above them, stretched along the front chosen for the British assault, were nine fortified villages, interspersed with specially built "redoubts", strong-points of dug-outs and trenches, each covering an area the size of Piccadilly Circus. There were also half a dozen dense woods and approximately 1000 machine-gun posts. At a rough estimate, each machine-gun could produce the fire-power of 40 first-class riflemen firing in unison. From the

Christmas Day on the Somme. Half a million animals died with British forces in the course of the war.

perspective of the British, however, this was irrelevant. Sustained and concentrated artillery fire would simply obliterate them.

The bombardment

The broad objectives of the Somme offensive were the responsibility of Sir Douglas Haig as Commander-in-Chief of the BEF. The actual task of carrying out the operation, however, fell upon the shoulders of Sir Henry Rawlinson, Commander of the Fourth Army, which would do all the actual fighting apart from the diversionary attack on Gommecourt. Rawlinson, a life-long infantryman, placed his faith not in his infantry, whom he distrusted as recently recruited amateurs, but in the power of the artillery, a branch of the service of which he knew little. His basic assumption was very simple: assemble every gun you can get hold of and inflict upon your enemy's position the heaviest and longest bombardment you can manage. This should, by definition, destroy the enemy defences and leave it open to the infantry to walk across and take possession. Then repeat the process, and so on.

Wise after the event, the British "Official History" noted waspishly that:

> "The problem facing the allies was, in fact, that of storming a fortress in which, according to history and precedent, there should be a main assault on the largest breach (or weakest spot), several subsidiary ones on minor breaches – which must be strong enough to be converted into main assaults and carried through – and false attacks."

In other words, the directing command, having studied the ground, should have positioned artillery *unequally* along the front, concentrating it around points where a break-through might be made. In fact, what happened was that guns were spaced evenly all the way along the front. The British "Official History" concedes:

> "It must be admitted that the problems of semi-siege warfare and the large concentration of guns necessary for the attack of great field defences had never been studied in practice by the General Staff . . .".

The British offensives of 1915 had been seriously hampered by a shell shortage. This time there was no shortage, in *quantity*. When the bombardment started on 24th June, 1916, there was a gun, howitzer or mortar for every 50 feet of the German front line. Compared with the Battle of Loos, the greatest previous bombardment attempted by British artillery, there would be twice as many guns and six times as many shells. In the course of the next week, British gunners would fire more rounds than they had in the entire first year of fighting.

The bombardment was organized according to a strict routine. Each morning there would be all-out, non-stop firing for 80 minutes. (On the morning of the attack this would be cut to 65 minutes, the idea being that any surviving Germans would remain crouching underground, waiting for the last 15 minutes of *Trommelfeuer* – drum-fire – and fearing that its absence was just a ruse to lure them out of safety.) The bombardment then continued at a more measured pace through the rest of the day until nightfall, when half the guns rested and their place was taken by heavy machine-guns. These then aimed to harass the enemy's rear trenches while

Too few too late. British heavy artillery in action.

Artillery in action in the Fricourt-Mametz area, August 1916.

he tried to bring up hot food, ammunition and relief troops under cover of dark. So much for the theory. In practice, the British bombardment had a number of crucial shortcomings.

Firstly, most (60%) of the British guns were 18-pounders. Their main task was to destroy barbed wire entanglements by firing shrapnel shells, which exploded in mid-air scattering small steel balls, as a shot-gun does pellets. The problem was that the shrapnel shells needed to explode at exactly the right height above the wire. If the fuse was set to explode too soon, most of the charge spread out harmlessly above its target; if set too late, the force of the explosion was absorbed by the ground. Given the lack of experience general among the artillery (some units had only received their guns when they actually arrived in France), it was unrealistic to expect a high standard of accuracy.

Secondly, the Brtitish lacked sufficient heavy guns, which were essential for destroying deep dug-outs. In fact, they had only 34 guns above 9.2 inches calibre and half of these had been borrowed from the French. And thirdly, the determination to build up an adequate stock-pile of ammunition had led to intense pressure on manufacturers and a resultant loss of quality. Some estimates put the proportion of "duds" as high as one third.

The sound of the bombardment could be heard quite plainly, right across the Channel in England itself. And the troops were cheered to think that their advance was being

Firepower. A heavy shell bursting during the Battle of the Somme.

prepared by such a majestic and relentless demonstration of power. Lt Adrian Stephen, an artillery officer, was positively inspired by the immense roar. He wrote in his diary:

"... wonderful music – the mightiest I ever heard. It seemed to throb into every vein, beating up and down, and yet never quite reaching a climax.... And then at last, ten minutes before zero, the guns opened their lungs. The climax had been reached. One felt inclined to laugh with the sheer exhilaration of it. After all it was our voice, the voice of a whole empire at war." (Quoted in S. Everett, *World War I*)

In the week that the bombardment lasted, 1,437 British guns fired 1,508,652 shells, about half of the stock-pile. It was to prove insufficient. Private George Coppard of the 37th Machine Gun Company surveyed the German front line on 2nd July, 24 hours after the initial assault:

"The German wire was so dense that daylight could barely be seen through it. The German faith in massed wire had paid off. How did our planners imagine that Tommies, having survived all other hazards . . . would get through the German wire? A vast amount of artillery fire was directed against the enemy wire before 1st July but it was largely wasted effort. In my opinion the German troops were in no way superior to the British. What was superior was the enemy trench system, built in thorough German fashion and defended by large numbers of machine-guns. What I saw on the morning of 2nd July made it clear that our chaps could only reach the wire – and then die." (George Coppard, *With a Machine-Gun to Cambrai*)

The military historian John Keegan summarizes the British failure as follows:

"... the great Somme bombardment, for all its sound and fury, was inadequate to the task those who planned it expected of it. The shells which the British guns had fired at the German trenches . . . were the wrong sort of projectile for the job and often badly made. And . . . the British . . . gunners, many of them amateurs, had largely to guess at where their real targets, the German machine-gun crews, were hidden and then very often lacked the skill to put a shell where they wanted it to fall." (John Keegan, *The Face of Battle*)

We've got them too! A Vickers machine-gun in action near Ovillers. Note the protective gas masks.

The advance Rawlinson was confident that the artillery bombardment would both destroy the German barbed wire and trenches and disable their defenders. Haig, to give him his due, did urge Rawlinson to shorten the bombardment so that the Germans should have less certain warning that this was indeed the great offensive of the year; to send out patrols periodically to check that the German defences had been adequately damaged, and to continue the bombardment if not; and to order his troops to rush the German line as soon as the barrage lifted. Rawlinson ignored these suggestions and, in deference to his expertise as a commander of infantrymen, Haig the cavalryman did not give him a direct order to adopt them. Having brushed aside the cautions of his superior, Rawlinson seemed similarly confident when dealing with the same fears raised by his Corps and Divisional commanders. They were infected with his optimism and stifled their doubts.

If Rawlinson demonstrated complete faith in his artillery, he left no doubt either of his strictly limited confidence in his infantry – who were, after all, the ones who would be doing the actual attacking. Basically, they were to be treated like

Weighed down. An infantryman in marching order was expected to advance at no more than two miles per hour.

robots, incapable of adapting to changing circumstances or of taking the initiative. When the bombardment stopped, they were to advance in waves into No Man's Land, each man five yards from his neighbour, each wave departing after an interval of one minute. Marching at a steady pace of 100 yards every two minutes – less than 2 m.p.h., half normal walking speed – they were forbidden to run until within 20 yards of the enemy, lest they lose formation or become too exhausted to fight. They were likewise forbidden to cheer or shout, lest they alert the enemy to their advance. Nor were they to delay for wounded comrades, who would swiftly be attended by medical orderlies.

Running, helping the wounded or even shouting were, in any case, not likely to recommend themselves to men carrying a minimum of 66 pounds of kit – a burden equal to roughly half their own body-weight. Even an army mule was expected to carry only a third of its own weight. As the "Official History" was later to concede, this "made it difficult to get out of a trench, impossible to move much quicker than a slow walk or to rise and lie down quickly".

The typical first-wave infantryman carried, as well as his packs containing clothes, iron rations, personal effects, field dressings and iodine and cleaning materials for his rifle and equipment, the following impedimenta: rifle, bayonet and 200 bullets; two gas helmets (for different kinds of gas), goggles and a steel helmet; two grenades and a flare for signalling; two empty sandbags, an entrenching-tool and a pair of wire-cutters; a water-bottle and ground-sheet.

Men in the following waves carried such additional burdens as signalling equipment, "duckboards" to lay down as instant pathways, and rolls of barbed wire and metal stakes to erect instant fortifications on captured positions. In training sessions most of these men had not even carried their full packs, let alone any additional equipment.

Had the bulk of the attacking troops been preceded by small groups of skirmishers, picked men, unburdened by equipment and suitably armed with bombs for clearing out trenches, their chances of success might have been a great deal higher. Committed as they were to plodding mechanically across No Man's Land, the infantry found themselves faced with no alternative to going forward to be slaughtered. Sergeant Jim Myers of the Machine Gun Corps, serving in the 31st Division, observed bitterly:

"The biggest mistake that was made on manoeuvres and

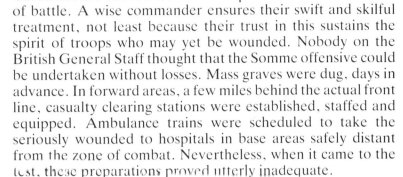

training was that we were never told what to do in case of failure. All that time we'd gone backwards and forwards, training, doing it over and over again like clockwork, and then when we had to advance, when it came to the bit, we didn't know what to do! Nothing seemed to be arranged in case of failure. (Quoted in Lyn Macdonald, *Somme*)

Could more lives have been saved?

Casualties are the inevitable accompaniment of the violence of battle. A wise commander ensures their swift and skilful treatment, not least because their trust in this sustains the spirit of troops who may yet be wounded. Nobody on the British General Staff thought that the Somme offensive could be undertaken without losses. Mass graves were dug, days in advance. In forward areas, a few miles behind the actual front line, casualty clearing stations were established, staffed and equipped. Ambulance trains were scheduled to take the seriously wounded to hospitals in base areas safely distant from the zone of combat. Nevertheless, when it came to the test, these preparations proved utterly inadequate.

Most Great War casualties were caused by artillery. In many cases men were simply blown to pieces. The Thiepval memorial records the names of more than 73,000 men whose remains were never recovered. However, on 1st July, 1916, the British tactics of calm advance into heavy machine-gun fire led to an unusually high proportion of casualties from bullet-wounds. Since the men were strictly forbidden to aid fallen comrades, the wounded were left to lie in No Man's Land until stretcher-bearers could carry them to their first point of assistance, the regimental field aid post, where they could be sedated and bandaged. Then they could be transferred to a casualty clearing station for more skilled treatment and, if necessary, major surgery. Here the medical staff would practise the testing art of "triage", dividing incoming wounded into three categories – those lightly wounded enough to be sent elsewhere, those seriously wounded enough to need extensive and immediate care but fit enough to benefit from it, and those who could only be comforted and left to die. The proportion of those in the third category, and the treatment they got, depended largely on the number received in any one period of time. At best they were few and tenderly treated – washed, fed and sedated out of pain and awareness of their approaching death. At worst they were put to one side while hard-pressed staff gave their time and skill to those who could be saved.

Comrades. Half an hour after this picture was taken, the man being carried to a dressing station had, in fact, died of his wounds.

There was an even worse fate – to be wounded in No Man's

Land and left to die there, alone and in agony. On 1st July, 1916, thousands were. Many pleaded with passing comrades to put them out of their pain.

Each battalion, sending about 800 men into action, had 32 stretcher-bearers, capable of carrying 16 wounded between them. The casualty rate on 1st July would have overwhelmed supermen.

It is estimated that about a third of the wounds inflicted on the first-line troops of the great assault were penetrations of the chest or abdomen or fractures of the thigh or skull. The damage was critical but, given skilled treatment, might not prove fatal. Had these men not lain out on the battlefield for hours, and in many cases days, after being wounded, perhaps as many as 6,000 or 7,000 additional lives might have been saved. And perhaps not, because the medical facilities behind the lines failed to cope with the tens of thousands who did reach them.

Why did the French succeed?

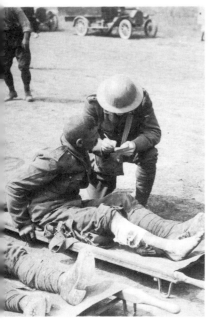

Practical Christianity. A chaplain takes notes of the names of the wounded to reassure their relatives. July 1916.

On 1st July, 1916, the five French divisions, attacking on an eight-mile front to the south of the river Somme, where the British and French lines joined, took four-fifths of their objectives in the course of the day, as well as twice as many prisoners as the British. Why?

The French had nearly four times as many heavy guns as the British for each mile of front that they were attacking. They therefore inflicted far more damage on the German dug-outs and their occupants. Secondly, the French launched their assault at 9.30 a.m., two hours later than the British. As the Germans were by then fully engaged with the British action, the French attack had the further advantage of surprise.

The French did not use the wave system but sent all their men forward in small groups, one moving while another gave it covering fire. This "fire and movement" system was well-known to the British, but thought to be beyond the capacity of raw troops.

The French lost fewer men than the Germans they were attacking. The British lost seven times as many.

Why did men fight?

There are really three questions to be answered. Why did men join the army? How did they learn to face death and kill others? How were they able to endure such terrible conditions for so long?

Recruitment – why did men join up?

"My very Dear Boy

. . . you never could mean what you put in your letter on Sunday . . . and what cause have you for such a Low Life . . . you have as good home as any one else in our station . . . you know you are the Great Hope of the Family . . . there are plenty of things steady young men can do when they can read and write as you can . . . [the Army] is a refuge for all idle people . . . I shall name it to no one for I am ashamed to think of it . . . I would rather bury you than see you in a red coat . . ." (Quoted in Victor Bonham Carter, *Soldier True*)

William Robertson had enlisted as a private soldier in 1877. Those words were his mother's reaction to the terrible news. Uniquely, Robertson rose from private to Field-Marshal and Chief of the Imperial General Staff (1916-18). No doubt his mother learned to change her mind. But her first response was typical of the respectable classes of Victorian England. "Everyone" knew that soldiers drank (heavily) and swore (profanely); above all, their way of life – mobile, dangerous, cut off from society – prevented them from enjoying that ideal of the period, a settled home.

The Boer War (1899-1902) called forth tens of thousands of volunteers. Attitudes began to change. That boy in uniform might be your son, brother or husband. It was the first war whose dead were widely commemorated by memorials raised by public subscription. Soldiering began to be respectable.

One outcome was the reorganization of the Volunteer movement. "Volunteer" rifle companies dated back to the 1860s, when Britain was seized by the fear of a French invasion. Massive forts were built to guard the mouth of the Thames. Coastal defences were strengthened. And thousands gave up their evenings and weekends to don uniforms and practise drill. When the war-scare passed, the Volunteer rifle companies carried on, as a sort of mildly eccentric, comic-opera pastime which offered the romance and glamour of soldiering without the taint of vice, or the possibility of real danger.

In 1908 the Volunteers were reformed to become the "Territorials", and their training was brought up nearer to the standard of the Regulars. By 1910 there were some 250,000 of these "Saturday Night Soldiers", meeting weekly in village and neighbourhood Drill Halls. Their terms of engagement did not oblige them to fight overseas, but when asked to do so on the outbreak of hostilities in 1914, over 90% agreed without hesitation. If the Regulars were to provide the BEF, which represented the main British military effort in 1914, it was Territorials, rushed out as reinforcements, who were to bear the burden of conflict in 1915.

Lord Kitchener first foresaw that the war would be a long one: at least three years in his estimation. This clearly conflicted with the "over by Christmas" mood of the general public, but such was the prestige of the colonial hero that his words took immediate effect as he appealed for a "First 100,000". Parliament passed a bill to authorize the recruitment of 500,000 men to form 18 new divisions. In fact, 30 divisions were to be raised and 2,250,000 men to volunteer before it was necessary to introduce conscription.

The response to Kitchener's summons to arms was overwhelming, but people's motives were mixed: pride in country and Empire; a desire to stand beside the embattled BEF; a thirst for travel and adventure; the glamour of a uniform; escape from debt or a nagging wife. Sometimes a lead was given by an employer or a land-owner, or his eldest son. More often men simply followed their mates. According to William Gallacher, a Scottish trade unionist who became one of the only two Communist MPs to sit in Parliament in modern times, the real motives were

". . . the wild excitement, the illusion of wonderful adventure and the actual break in the deadly monotony of working-class life. Thousands went flocking to the colours in the first days, not because of any 'love of country', not because of any high feeling of 'patriotism' but because of the new, strange and thrilling life that lay before them." (Quoted in Norman Longmate, *Milestones in Working Class History*)

In theory, they had to pass a strict medical inspection. Many were shown how to cheat – the under-weight, the under-

height and the under-age. Some, for pressing personal
reasons, dyed their hair or used false names. The recruiting
sergeants, who were paid by results, knew when to turn a
blind eye.

Private Ernest Atkins of the King's Royal Rifle Corps
remembered how he and his friend were re-classified once
they had been accepted for service:

> "In front of me was my pal Jock . . . . The doctor said,
> 'What are you down "Home Service" for?' Jock replied,
> 'I've lost one ear drum and am slightly deaf in the other.'
> The doctor said, 'Splendid, you won't be troubled with the
> bombardments. A1' Then he looked me up and down.
> 'And what is the matter with a great fellow like you?' I said,
> 'Nothing, except the army won't pass me for overseas on
> account of my eyesight.' He said, 'Well, if you can't see
> them, they will damn soon see you! A1." (Quoted in
> Moynihan (ed.) *People at War 1914-1918*)

The army took many who, on strict medical grounds, were
unfit for service. It also transformed many sickly fellows into
fit and active young men. Thousands of slum-dwellers
benefited in a startling way from the army's regular, adequate
meals, fresh air and strenuous exercise. On their first leave
after "basic training" they strode erect to their old homes,
visibly healthier, stronger and more confident of their worth
as men than they had ever been in their lives. By their very
example they inspired others to join, to work upon themselves the same miraculous transformation.

In Liverpool Lord Derby, "The King of Lancashire",
appealed to the young men of the city to form their own unit.
The War Office responded with a pledge that, wherever
possible, groups of young men who joined up together would
be assigned to the same units. Thus were born the "Pals'
Battalions". Manchester raised no fewer than 15, but Hull, a
much smaller city, also raised an entire brigade – four
battalions. "The Commercials" came from the city's business
offices; a second battalion was composed of "Tradesmen"
and a third of "Sportsmen". The fourth called themselves
simply "T'Others". The catastrophe of the Somme offensive,
which annihilated whole brigades, brought such concentrated
misery to whole communities that Pals' Battalions were
thenceforth abandoned.

Many came in response to Kitchener's stern gaze. Others
needed to be able to answer the child's innocent accusation –

"What did you do in the Great War, Daddy?" Others still, perhaps no less courageous for their reluctance, were more or less hounded in, as happened to Private Martin:

> "I hated war and the thought of killing anyone but I lived in a small village and, when all the others had gone, people started asking me when I would be going. I got fed up with this and joined up but was determined to be a non-combatant. I tried to join the RAMC [Royal Army Medical Corps] but could not get in so I finished up as a stretcher-bearer in the infantry." (Quoted in Middlebrook, *The First Day on the Somme*)

Some, of course, refused absolutely, on moral or religious grounds, to have anything to do with the armed services. The law allowed this, though the manner of its application depended on the whims of local appeals tribunals which were supposed to screen the grounds of men's refusal to serve. Many would-be "conscientious objectors" capitulated under interrogation and agreed to accept a non-combatant role in a hospital or working on the land. Some 3,000 refused absolutely to do anything that might contribute to the war effort and were consequently imprisoned. Of these, about 70 died as a result of the treatment they suffered.

Combat – how did men learn to fight?

The Regulars faced the prospect of battle with few qualms. According to Lieutenant-General Sir Tom Bridges:

> ". . . the 2nd Cavalry Brigade to which I belonged was in a high state of efficiency and was quite ready to fight anybody. There was no hatred of Germany but in the true mercenary spirit we would equally readily have fought the French. Our motto was, "We'll do it. What is it?". (Lt-Gen. Sir Tom Bridges, *Alarms and Excursions*)

The men of the "New Army" contrasted dramatically with this cool, professional detachment. Their outlook was amateur in every sense of the word, untrained, high-spirited, adventurous. Initially their training was a matter of sorting out a cheerful chaos. The normal army administration had been quite overwhelmed by the flood of volunteers. Even after the first muddle had been dealt with and roughly the right men found themselves in roughly the right barracks or temporary camps, they still lacked most of the things needed to turn civilians into soldiers – uniforms, weapons and instructors who did know what soldiering was about. Many were surprised to find themselves dressing up in the blue serge usually associated with postmen. No matter, it was all a tremendous "lark" and they laughed and joked and drilled obediently and learned to fire disciplined volleys and thrust cleanly with their bayonet. Only at the front would they learn that a bayonet on the end of a rifle was useless in the confines of a muddy trench and that the most serviceable weapons were a grenade, a dagger and a home-made cosh.

Whatever made men join up, it was seldom the same thing that made them fight. The poet Robert Graves emphasized that:

> "There was no patriotism in the trenches. It was too remote a sentiment and rejected as fit only for civilians. A new arrival who talked patriotism would soon be told to cut it out . . . Great Britain was a quiet, easy place to get back to, out of the present foreign misery, but as a nation it was nothing." (Robert Graves, *Goodbye To All That*)

Hatred of the enemy, the negative side of patriotism, could be inflamed in the course of action as men sought personal revenge for close friends killed in battle – particularly where the enemy in question could be identified: a particular sniper or machine-gunner. Artillery, which killed far more men than all the snipers and machine-gunners put together, was somehow more impersonal, though not for Private Atkins:

> ". . . I had received a letter some days previously to say my brother had been killed. He was serving with the Royal Artillery and had been killed by a long-distance shell . . . . We were very close. There I am on the ground and crowds of Germans in front of me . . . . Suddenly I think of my brother and I will be revenged . . . . I settle my rifle in an easy position and start to shoot them down. This was the only time in the war that was mine and mine alone. At all

Waiting. Exhausted men snatch sleep in a trench.

other times, I was part of the war machine and killing was just part of the day's work, with no personal feelings." (Quoted in Moynihan (ed.), *People at War, 1914-1918*)

The source of the courage to go "over the top" is perhaps best illustrated by a letter written by Lt Eric Heaton on the eve of the battle of the Somme. Heaton was serving in the 16th (Public Schools) Battalion of the Middlesex Regiment, a battalion that was eventually to produce over 1,400 officers. As a very junior commander he was still acutely conscious of being a pupil in everything:

"This life abroad has taught me many things, chiefly the fine character of the British race to put up with hardships with wonderful cheerfulness."

His own fears were directed, not towards the enemy, but towards his own sense of inadequacy:

"I am writing this on the eve of my first action. Tomorrow we go to the attack in the greatest battle the British Army has ever fought. I cannot quite express my feeling on this night and I cannot tell you if it is God's will that I shall come through but if I fall in battle then I have no regrets save for my loved ones I leave behind. It is a great cause and I came out willingly to serve my King and Country. My greatest concern is that I may have the courage and determination necessary to lead my platoon well." (Quoted in Annette Tapert (ed.), *Despatches from the Heart*)

"Into Thy Hands, O Lord." Troops taking spiritual comfort before battle.

Lt Heaton was mortally wounded on 1st July, 1916. His concerns were probably typical of front-line officers: the grief of those at home, offset by a more immediate sense of responsibility for one's comrades.

Lt Harry Yoxall of the 18th King's Royal Rifle Corps took an unusually broad view of the conflict, perhaps because he was the son of an MP and therefore more aware of the war as a national struggle rather than a personal test:

> "Our losses are terrible but probably it is more economic of life to spend it freely now and avoid a long-drawn war of attrition with its steady wastage. I know how terrible the cost must seem to all of you who are waiting at home, because each time I lose a friend all the joy of living seems to go for a moment . . . . The only difficulty in facing death is the foreknowledge of the grief of one's people . . . . So if you at home can bear the cost we out here can endure the expenditure, even though it be of ourselves, very lightly. Remember that it is only by more sacrifices that we can save the sacrifices of the past two years from having been made in vain." (Quoted in Annette Tapert (ed.), *Despatches from the Heart*)

Lt Yoxall went on to win further promotion and the Military Cross. After the war he was to make a distinguished career in journalism.

The necessity of sacrifice was expressed even more forcefully by Lt William St Leger of the Coldstream Guards:

> "I hope to God the politicians in England will not betray us and make peace before we have absolutely crushed our enemies and made a repetition of this hellish business impossible. To make peace before this is done would be a criminal betrayal of the Living and the Dead. Modern war is hell and we must make a recurrence of it impossible for all generations, cost what it may . . . . Hundreds of thousands of brave men have still to lay down their lives, leaving ruined, desolate homes to mourn their loss. But over the graves the armies of Right and Civilisation will sweep invincibly on . . ." (Quoted in Moynihan (ed.) *People at War 1914-1918*)

Lt St Leger was later to win the Military Cross and to be killed in action in April 1918.

Lieutenants Heaton, Yoxall and St Leger were acutely aware of the responsibilities and meaning of leadership. And leadership is a prime focus of military training. It was not lacking on the Somme. From privates to colonels, there were outstanding acts of courage and defiance which inspired ordinary men to extraordinary actions. When men began to retreat without orders from a captured German strong-point on 1st July, Drummer Ritchie of the Seaforth Highlanders leapt onto the parapet of a captured trench and repeatedly sounded the "Charge", oblivious of German fire. He survived the action and the war and won the VC. When the 10th Battalion of the Green Howards left their trenches that same day, to be met by murderous machine-gun fire, Major Loudon-Shand strode into the open, pulling men after him until he was himself struck down. Propped up as he lay dying, he continued to urge his men forward until he lost the power of speech. He also won the VC.

Platoon and company commanders came, for the most part, from the public schools. They had been taught to expect to take a lead, to exercise responsibility, as the price of privilege, and to value traditions and taboos, rituals and rivalries. For them a regiment was a boarding-house writ large. They were supposed to radiate confidence, cheerfulness and courage. Most of them did. Their men, products of the state elementary schools, had likewise been taught that officers were by definition gentlemen and vice versa. They were to be obeyed and followed. And they were.

Officers and men, however far divided by their circumstances of birth and education, shared a common and unquestionable conviction: British was best. They learned to respect the Germans as brave fighters and even to sympathize with them as men with homes and families, suffering hardships like their own. But such feelings did little to diminish their commitment to the task in hand. They were seldom uplifted by visions of fighting for a more perfect world. Instead, a favourite sing-song dirge expressed their attitude far more concisely: "We're 'ere because we're 'ere because we're 'ere because . . .". As a moral stance it was singularly unthinking. But it was also well-nigh unbeatable.

Endurance In Robert Graves' opinion, two factors counted when it came to fighting: the discipline instilled by relentless training and the proud solidarity of the fighting unit. Training gave men unthinking reflexes which enabled them to react in a controlled way under the stress of battle. Group loyalty made them more afraid of letting down their comrades than of losing their limbs or their lives.

Training and regimental pride varied, leading Graves and his fellow trench-fighting instructors to develop their own ranking order of fighting capability:

"We decided that about a third of the troops in the BEF were dependable on all occasions . . . . About a third were variable . . . . The remainder were more or less untrustworthy; being put in positions of comparative safety they had about a quarter of the casualties that the best divisions had. It was a matter of pride to belong to one of the recognized best divisions – the 7th, the 29th, Guards, 1st Canadian, for instance . . . promotion, leave and the chance of a wound came quicker in them. The mess agreed that the most dependable British troops were the Midland county regiments, industrial Yorkshire and Lancashire troops and the Londoners. The Ulstermen, Lowland Scots and Northern English were pretty good. The Catholic Irish and the Highland Scots were not considered so good – they took unnecessary risks in trenches and had unnecessary casualties, and in battle, though they usually made their objective, they too often lost it in the counter-attack; without officers they were no good. English southern county regiments varied from good to very bad. All overseas troops were good." (Robert Graves, *Goodbye To All That*)

If units varied in their "reliability", so did individuals. Given the horrendous circumstances in which men had not just to fight occasionally but to live permanently, it is surprising only that desertions could be numbered in dozens rather than thousands. Invariably, desertion was the act of a mind at the end of its tether. It was made quite clear to men going over the top on 1st July that in the rear trenches there were armed military police who would "deal with" anyone moving in the wrong direction.

On three occasions Lt Bernard Martin served on Courts Martial dealing with cases of desertion. He was no lawyer himself, but recognized summary justice when he saw it:

"The evidence of desertion was always irrefutable, the accused being caught in the act – he should have been with his unit and had been found somewhere else. The verdict was certain, the punishment already determined – shot by a firing squad of his own unit [i.e. by his comrades]."

At first, such sentences scarcely troubled the young officer:

". . . the execution of a few miserable deserters seemed to me unimportant when the day before yesterday eight chaps in my platoon had been killed and as like as not there would be as many or more tomorrow."

But later he came to change his mind:

"As a general observation I'd say we PBI [Poor Bloody Infantry] at the front had no contempt for deserters such as we felt for Scrimshankers [men who hadn't volunteered] and Base-Wallahs [men with jobs safely away from the front]. Deserters had volunteered to serve King and Country, but when they came out found war was unlike what they had supposed and they just couldn't take it . . . . Others may have overcome fear at first with courage but their courage had worn thin, as courage always does in time: they'd generally cracked up and tried to get away without plan or hope. They deserved pity, not contempt." (Bernard Martin, *Poor Bloody Infantry*)

The overwhelming majority never even attempted to get away. They suffered and they stayed, together.

Experience turned some of the older soldiers into skilled amateur psychiatrists. Private Ernest Atkins recalled:

"As the younger lads started to come out I would be called for to calm them down if any casualties occurred. The best way was to put them to work and pretend to be hard. On one occasion a young lad was crying because his pal had been killed and he'd promised to look after him. What should he tell the boy's mother? 'Who said you were going to get home to tell his mother? Someone will be telling your mother if you don't get this trench built up. Come on now, let's get on with it.' Often they would work up a bit of resentment against my hard heart and that helped a lot. They didn't know how sorry I was for them." (Quoted in Moynihan (ed.), *People at War 1914-1918*)

For many, the Somme campaign marked a turning-point in their attitude to the war. Idealism died with their comrades, as Bert Chaney, an NCO with the Royal Signals, was fully aware:

Pep-talk. General de Lisle, Divisional Commander, addresses the 1st Lancashire Fusiliers on the eve of the Battle of the Somme, 29 June 1916.

"To our minds the generals would keep us out here until we were all killed, and although nobody thought of disobeying orders some of the originals continually grumbled at the way the war was going. We were proud of all the new guns, the new men coming out were just as enthusiastic as we had been originally, but after two years away from home we were beginning to think the war would never end. From now on the veterans, myself included, decided to do no more than was really necessary, following orders but if possible keeping out of harm's way. I have a feeling that many of the officers felt the same way." (Quoted in Moynihan (ed.), *People at War 1914-1918*)

Words and deeds were often far apart, as one officer made clear in a letter home:

"I can bear testimony to the splendid qualities of our troops, they are perhaps the biggest lot of grousers under the sun, but they have their grouse and finish with it and always fight well. No task is too great for them to undertake, but they must have their grouse with it, it is part of their lives." (Quoted in John Terraine, *Impacts of War 1914 and 1918*)

Comradeship could overcome many hardships and dangers. However, one test repeatedly pushed men to the limits of their endurance, as Private Sweeney of the 1st Lincolns confessed to his fiancée:

"I told you dear that I was happy, well so I am, but I think of my poor dear old chums who have fallen – I could cry. I have had to cry in the trench with one of my chums, poor old Jack Nokes, he has been out here since the very beginning of the war and has not received a scratch . . . . Poor lad, he died game, with his mother's name his last word. I cried like a child . . . . Ivy, I cannot tell you the horrors of this war. You cannot realise what it is like to see poor lads lying about with such terrible wounds and we cannot help them." (Quoted in Annette Tapert (ed.), *Despatches from the Heart*)

That passed the regimental censor. God only knows what he cut out.

Why did people support the war?

Were people conditioned to expect a war?

The decade before the outbreak of the Great War saw the final achievement of almost a century of educational effort in Britain – virtually 100% school attendance. The quality of education may have been poor. The tone was fiercely nationalistic. Robert Roberts, who grew up in Salford, remembered over-crowded classes, poorly qualified teachers, truancy and beatings. He also remembered Empire Day, when the children marched around the playground, sang patriotic songs and saluted the Union Jack. Standing out in his memory, too, was the coronation of King George V in 1911, when a local charity paid for every child to receive a present of chocolate in a special gift box, with a portrait of the King on it. However little British children may have learned at school, whether in a smoky slum or a remote village, they would certainly know that they were citizens of the largest and greatest Empire the world had ever seen, and that they owed a duty of loyalty to the King-Emperor who ruled over it. The public schools went further and introduced specifically military training. Almost every major school had its own OTC (Officer Training Corps), which taught young men the elements of drill, map-reading and musketry and induced in them the habit of command. When war broke out there were literally thousands of potential platoon commanders ready to be pressed into service.

The intense patriotism engendered by the education system was reinforced by the popular press, cheap magazines and best-selling novels, many of which fantasized about a future war in Europe where the enemy was invariably the Kaiser's Germany. *The Riddle of the Sands*, by the Boer War hero Erskine Childers, told the thrilling story of two English yachtsmen in the Baltic who stumbled across secret German invasion preparations. William Le Queux's *The Invasion of 1910* told British readers what their national nightmare – occupation by a German army – would actually be like. There was no active conspiracy to prepare the British people for war, but the foundations for great national sacrifices were being laid nonetheless.

Another patriotic institution grew directly out of the Boer War. Robert Baden-Powell, the heroic commander of the besieged city of Mafeking, had made extensive use of boy volunteers as message runners during the siege. When in 1908 he decided to organize a movement for young lads which would give them opportunities for healthy exercise and service to the community, it was quite natural that he should call its members "Boy Scouts". His immense national prestige made the new organization a brilliant success from the start, quickly attracting thousands of fervent members. German observers certainly saw it as a para-military formation, however innocent of aggression its activities were in practice. Perhaps they were right. Over 10,000 scouts were to be killed serving their country during the Great War. Eleven were to win the VC.

War when it came was not, therefore, entirely unexpected. Nor was it viewed as an essentially barbaric throw-back to a more primitive era. All the great powers of Europe had acquired their overseas empires by force, and held them by the threat of its use. War was still regarded as a normal way in which states settled their differences. The USA had fought Spain in 1898, Russia had fought Japan in 1904-5, Italy and various Balkan states had fought the Ottoman Empire in 1911-12. True, an international conference had been convened at the Hague in 1907-8 to arrange a universal code of rules for the treatment of prisoners, non-combatants, etc, but this very exercise revealed that the participating delegations all regarded war as a more or less natural and permanent feature of the international landscape, to be "civilized" rather than abolished.

The real point was, of course, that the crowds on the streets of London, Paris, Berlin and Vienna, who cheered the outbreak of war in 1914, had not the slightest conception of the sort of conflict they were getting into – carnage and destruction on a scale unprecedented in the history of Europe. They saw before them the promise of a great adventure and a noble cause. On the day war was declared, Michael MacDonagh, a writer for the *The Times*, observed people in the streets around the House of Commons:

"Parliament St. and Whitehall were thronged with people highly excited and rather boisterous. A brilliant sun shone in a cloudless sky. Young men in straw hats were in the majority. Girls in light calico dresses were numerous. All were already touched with war fever. They regarded their country as a crusader – redressing all wrongs and bringing freedom to oppressed nations. Cries of 'Down with Germany!' were raised. The singing of patriotic songs such

A close one! Only in 1916 did all British troops acquire the protection of "tin hats".

as 'Rule Britannia', 'The Red, White and Blue' and also 'The Marseillaise' brought the crowds still closer in national companionship. They saw England radiant through the centuries, valiant and invincible and felt assured that so she shall appear for ever." (Michael MacDonagh, *In London During the Great War*)

Did everyone support the war? Recruiting sergeants appealed to British subjects to serve their King and, when they agreed to do so, gave them "the King's shilling" in token of their pledge. The King, for his part, also undertook enthusiastically to do his duty. George V had been trained as a professional naval officer and had served for more than a decade with the fleet. A conventional and unimaginative man, he was sincere and conscientious in his concern to lead by example. Conscious of the impact that alcohol could have on industrial output, he swore to give up drink for the duration of the war. Few even of his courtiers followed his example. He visited factories, training camps and men at the front and in hospital. He personally decorated thousands, and did not flinch, as Haig did, from the hideously wounded. As early as September 1914, Sir George Arthur, an eminent civil servant, recorded a sardonic royal witticism provoked by the fortunes of war:

> ". . . the King is concerned with nothing except winning the war; even when Winston Churchill casually remarked that if Buckingham Palace were bombed by a Zeppelin it would have a very stimulating effect upon the people, the King only mildly suggested that it might have a depressing effect upon him." (Sir George Arthur, *Further Letters of a Man of No Importance*)

The King's eldest son and heir, the Prince of Wales, likewise took a visibly keen interest in the conduct of the war, though he evidently found his role frustrating, as Bernard Martin cryptically noted in his diary:

> "In tent opposite ours HRH the Prince of Wales . . . . He's not allowed near any fighting of course, chap on his staff says he's unconventional, impatient of old fogeys, wants to be up-to-date, forward-looking. We watched his coming and going, talking and laughing with his staff. Sometimes he nodded our way affably. We concluded he's indignant at this Cook's Tour, a sham pretence to make people at home believe he's doing his bit with us." (Bernard Martin, *Poor Bloody Infantry*)

The Prince's main military contribution may have been handing out hand made cigarettes to astonished Tommies, but the photographs of him which were published at home made a significant contribution to the war effort. They represented a clear statement that *all* the King's subjects, from his own son downwards, had their part to play.

Where royalty led, the aristocracy followed, directing their butlers, grooms, gardeners and tenants to join up. They also directed their sons to do so. Hundreds of thousands of working-class families and a few thousand aristocratic families lost their heirs and successors. In proportion, the aristocratic families suffered the heavier losses. While the gentlemen drilled and fought, their ladies organized committees, raised funds, nursed convalescents and supervised the production of mountains of "comforts" for the troops in the field. In the course of the war these were to amount to 1,742,947 mufflers, 1,574,155 pairs of mittens, 3,607,059 pairs of socks and 6,145,673 hospital bags. Voluntary organizations also paid for over 12,000,000 bandages, 45,000,000 dressings, 16,000,000 books and 232,000,000 cigarettes. Every sock knitted, every cigarette paid for, represented time, effort and involvement, and, to that extent, strengthened commitment to the cause of victory.

Leadership by example spread throughout the social hierarchy. In Liverpool it was Lord Derby who appealed for the first "Pals' Battalion". In nearby Accrington it was the local mayor. Across the Pennines in Hull it was a local schoolmaster. As the BEF suffered reverses, as the lists of casualties lengthened, local leaders of hard-hit communities saw it as one of their prime duties to maintain popular support for the war. Local newspaper editors attempted to turn grief into pride by publishing a weekly "Roll of Honour" featuring stiff studio portraits of "the Fallen".

The solidarity of the respectable classes in their support for the war made the prospects dim indeed for any peace movement among their social inferiors. Nevertheless there were times and places where the populace did not appear to be 100% behind "the boys at the front". On "Red Clydeside" a small group of Marxist union leaders was able to organize a series of strikes among skilled engineering workers. Their grievances, however, were strictly economic – protests against rising rents and food prices and objections to the employment of women workers or the introduction of new machinery from America. All attempts to turn their discontents into a general anti-war movement failed miserably. And Glasgow as a whole was to supply no fewer than 200,000 men for His Majesty's forces – one in 40 of all who served from Britain and the entire Empire

Were people the victims of propaganda?

The army was to learn by experience that the press could be a two-edged weapon. In the autumn of 1914 every major newspaper was solidly behind the war. The uncritical support of the press, coupled with the sensationalist tone of much of its reporting, undoubtedly helped to swell the tide of volunteers, as the historian Correlli Barnett has emphasized:

> "The existence of the masses was boring, monotonous and insecure, their leisure short . . . their emotional and sexual life deprived and repressed. Even before the war, contemplation of their country's strength and glory had served to give . . . colour and fulfilment to the narrow lives of the lower-middle and working-classes . . . . These people . . . had no roots, no secure emotional foundations, no personal independence, no education but the ability haltingly to read and write. They had not the ability to analyze and reason or the information by which such an ability could form sound judgments. Instead they were ruled by emotion and romance. Men like Pearson and Harmsworth had grown rich by providing them with reading matter: nothing boringly factual or closely argued, of course, but highly coloured and exciting stuff . . . . The ever-responsive popular press gave its readers what they wanted: atrocity stories by the columnful . . ." (Correlli Barnett, "The Illogical Promise" in G.A. Panichas (ed.), *Promise of Greatness*)

However, journalists also have the professional habit of asking awkward questions, exposing what other people would rather have covered up. In the course of 1915, Col. Repington, military correspondent of *The Times*, revealed that the operations of the BEF had been seriously hampered by shortages of ammunition. The "shell scandal" became a major political issue, leading to the creation of a new Ministry of Munitions headed by the dynamic David Lloyd George. Given that the outcome was a greatly expanded supply of war material (albeit much of it of dubious quality), the army could scarcely complain about this act of "exposure". Senior officers were much less happy about the editorial line taken by Horatio Bottomley's *John Bull*, an unashamedly populist magazine which became the largest-selling journal in Britain.

Are YOU in this?

Doing Your Bit? Even the Boy Scout (centre) helps out – not surprisingly in a poster designed by Baden-Powell, founder of the Boy Scouts and himself a former soldier and war hero.

"We'll get 'em!" French poster for national savings shows an eager "joilu".

2ᴱ EMPRUNT
DE
LA DEFENSE NATIONALE

Souscrives

Bottomley, though personally a scoundrel and a cynical manipulator of ordinary people's simple faith in the printed word, saw that there was a great deal of mileage to be got out of publicizing the grouses and grievances of the common soldier. Officers repeatedly ordered the confiscation of *John Bull* in the trenches – but to little avail.

The army generally took the view that war should be left to the professionals. Generals disliked the "interference" of politicians and regarded the "snooping" of journalists with positive disgust. As far as the generals were concerned, the official communiqués of events telegraphed from GHQ contained all the facts that journalists or their readers needed to know. Haig was, however, somewhat jolted by a confrontation with a group of Fleet Street correspondents when Philip Gibbs of the *Daily Telegraph* told him bluntly that he:

". . . could not conduct his war in secret, as though the people at home, whose sons and husbands were fighting and dying, had no concern in the matter. The spirit of the fighting men, and the driving power behind the armies, depended upon the support of the whole people and their continuing loyalties." (Quoted in Lyn Macdonald, *Somme*)

Haig's response was a master-stroke. Henceforth approved correspondents were to be given uniforms, official accommodation, personal liaison officers to censor their despatches in the interests of military security, and access to the services of no less a person than the King's Messenger to carry their copy daily to London. As a crowning touch they were also given the privilege of wearing the green armbands of the Intelligence Service. The journalists responded to the army's "generosity" by putting the "news" in the most positive manner possible, invariably stressing ground gained rather than men lost.

Already on 1st July evening papers in London carried reports of the offensive – optimistic, short on detail and quite often wrong. The *Evening News*, for example, carried a piece from the Reuter's correspondent which proclaimed that the German front line had been taken, along with many prisoners, at small loss to the British. On Sunday, 2nd July, Britain's biggest-selling paper, *The News of the World*, reassured its readers that "The Day Goes Well for our Heroic

Troops" and incorrectly informed them that Serre and La Boisselle had been taken. In its commentary on the sparsely worded official communiqués, the paper revealed that it had already accepted that the offensive was not going to lead to any breakthrough, but was essentially part of a strategy of attrition, grinding down enemy resistance:

> "Of far more consequence than any mere gain of ground is the work of inflicting upon the enemy heavier losses than those he inflicts upon us. When the enemy has had his fill of punishment he must yield ground."

On Monday, 3rd, *The Daily Express* claimed that the British had taken 9,500 prisoners (in fact, the figure was nearer 2,000), although it did also carry an ominous hint of what was to come: "The New Tactics – Warnings Against Undue Optimism". It was *The Times* which eventually gave the most accurate account of the first day's fighting – based on the German official communiqué published in the press in neutral European countries.

Front-line troops regarded newspaper coverage of the war with derision, recognizing that its main purpose was to keep up the morale of civilians, rather than to give accurate or realistic accounts of events and conditions in the battle zone. In writing home, soldiers repeatedly warned their relatives that what they read in the papers was simply rubbish. Sometimes, it must be admitted, the soldiers were themselves responsible for this. When Bernard Martin and a fellow officer were ordered to show a visiting journalist round the front line, they took him instead to a wrecked factory nearly a mile away from it, where they made him, quite unnecessarily, crawl about in the rubble until he was out of breath. They then pretended to hear gas shells and made him put his mask on. They rounded off the tour with a selection of tall stories and returned him to "safety" well satisfied with their afternoon's amusement. "The real joke came a fortnight later in a London daily newspaper – the writer had been in the front line, under shell fire and the threat of snipers . . .". Truly, as Senator Harman Johnson was to remark in 1917, "The first casualty in war is truth."

Their own worst enemies?

Correlli Barnett has argued persuasively that the civilian masses of Europe had only themselves to blame for the prolongation of the Great War. His argument starts from the premise that the war itself was "a meaningless accident":

> "Austria alone went to war deliberately to achieve a limited and perfectly rational objective: the crushing of Serbia and the ending of the unrest Serbia had encouraged among Austria's south Slav peoples. Every other nation in 1914 entered the war for negative reasons – not in pursuit of aims, but because of obligations and fear of others." ("The Illogical Promise", in G.A. Panichas (ed.), *Promise of Greatness*)

Once started, however, the war became uncontrollable because its conduct released "the quenchless hatred of the common man" and required his continuing support:

> ". . . industrial mobilization meant that ardent participation of the masses in the war had to be enlisted. It could not be a 'Cabinet' war, a relatively precise instrument of realistic policy firmly under the control of the cool judgment of statesmen. Governments therefore had to meet the uncaged little man half way: the little man had to be flattered, encouraged, filled with a sense of his importance, of the glory and righteousness of the cause and of the criminal depravity of the enemy."

The inflammation of popular hatred made it impossible for statesmen on either side to seek a rational compromise peace. Meanwhile it was the soldiers who suffered, "placed between the enemy barbed wire and machine guns in front and their relatives behind demanding victory at all costs".

The carnage of 1916 and the long, hard winter of 1916-17, Barnett suggests, changed the outlook of the combatant nations. They needed to look forward not merely to victory, but to something that would justify and redeem the slaughter and sacrifice. On the Allied side it therefore became the war to end war itself.

The war ended when it did, only because Germany was

temporarily exhausted. Her territory had not been invaded. Her future capacity for war had not been destroyed. The Allied peacemakers were faced with the problem of constructing a stable post-war settlement based on two contradictory principles – punishing Germany without mercy and ushering in an era of sweetness and light among all nations. They were also supposed to settle the tedious practical problems of dozens of territorial boundary disputes while securing the rights of minority peoples. Barnett concludes by summarizing the, to him, disastrous outcomes of popular involvement in international affairs:

> "the nature of the Great War . . . and the nature of the peace . . . are the immediate consequences of the uncaging of the little man, the eruption of mass opinion as a force of which statesmen must take continuous account. This eruption marks the advent of the irrational, of fantasy and ignorance, into the higher conduct of human affairs to a degree never before seen in modern time . . . . The pattern established during the Great War is still with us: great international questions are seen in simple moralistic and idealistic terms, as emotional crusades; statesmen still find their freedom to strike realistic bargains hampered by the . . . expectations at home . . . statesmen have developed the double personality: the actor-statesman, all ideals and generalised goodness for the television, and the real statesman behind the TV make-up. The influence of the masses has introduced falsity, as well as rigidity, into international affairs."

Perhaps so, but when the armistice came at last, there were few in Britain who voiced the thought that a victory so dearly won had not, after all, been worth it.

Rest in Peace. Grave of an unknown British soldier killed in the Somme campaign, September 1916.

Further reading

John Brophy and Eric Partridge, *The Long Trail: Soldiers' Songs and Slang 1914-1918*, Sphere 1969

D.S.V. Fosten and R.J. Marrion, *The British Army 1914-18*, Osprey 1978

Robert Graves, *Goodbye to All That*, Penguin ed. 1969

John Keegan, *The Face of Battle*, Penguin ed. 1978

Peter Liddle, *The Soldiers' War*, Blandford 1988

Lyn Macdonald, *Somme*, Papermac ed. 1984

Bernard Martin, *Poor Bloody Infantry*, John Murray 1987

Martin Middlebrook, *The First Day on the Somme*, Penguin ed. 1984

Michael Moynihan (ed.) *People at War 1914-18*, David & Charles 1988

Victor Neuburg *A Guide to the Western Front: A Companion for Travellers*, Penguin 1988

George A. Panichas (ed.) *Promise of Greatness*, Cassell 1968

Peter Slowe and Richard Woods, *Fields of Death*, Robert Hale 1986

Richard Tames, *The Great War*, Batsford 1984

A.J.P. Taylor, *The First World War: An Illustrated History*, Penguin ed. 1984

John Terraine, *The First World War*, Papermac ed. 1984

Index